THE JOURNEY TO ME

A 21-DAY MINDFULNESS WORKBOOK FOR KIDS

BY LAUREN PAX

ART BY EMILY HUNT

PRINTED IN THE UNITED STATES OF AMERICA
PUBLISHED BY BRAUGHLER BOOKS LLC., SPRINGBORO, OHIO

FIRST PRINTING, 2020

ISBN: 978-1-970063-86-8

LIBRARY OF CONGRESS CONTROL NUMBER: 2020924064

ORDERING INFORMATION: SPECIAL DISCOUNTS ARE AVAILABLE ON
QUANTITY PURCHASES BY BOOKSTORES, CORPORATIONS, ASSOCIATIONS,
AND OTHERS. FOR DETAILS, CONTACT THE PUBLISHER AT:

SALES@BRAUGHLERBOOKS.COM
OR AT 937-58-BOOKS

FOR QUESTIONS OR COMMENTS ABOUT THIS BOOK, PLEASE WRITE TO:
INFO@BRAUGHLERBOOKS.COM

hEY gROWN-UPS,

THANK YOU FOR ENTRUSTING US TO TAKE YOUR KIDDOS ON A MINDFULNESS JOURNEY THEY WON'T FORGET.

YOU PROBABLY AGREE THAT A REGULAR MINDFULNESS PRACTICE CAN MAKE A PRETTY INCREDIBLE IMPACT ON OUR WELLBEING... THAT IS, WHEN WE ACTUALLY MAKE THE TIME TO DO IT. THAT'S WHY WE'VE INCLUDED 21 DAYS OF ACTIVITIES FOR THE KIDS IN YOUR LIFE. WE CREATED THIS BOOK TO ENCOURAGE CHILDREN TO MAKE THIS DAILY PRACTICE A LONG-TERM HABIT, EVEN AFTER THEY'VE FINISHED THE BOOK.

WHEN CREATING THE JOURNEY TO ME, WE HAD A CLEAR VISION FOR HELPING KIDS SEE THE MAGNIFICENCE THAT IS IN EACH OF THEM. BY THE END OF THIS PRACTICE, WE'RE SURE THEY WILL SEE THE GOLD THAT'S BEEN INSIDE THEM ALL ALONG.

THESE DAILY ACTIVITIES CAN EVEN COME IN HANDY FOR US ADULTS. SO GO AHEAD, JOIN IN ON THE FUN.

THERE'S MORE FUN WAITING FOR YOU AND THE KIDS... FIND US ON INSTAGRAM, FACEBOOK AND JOURNEYTOMEBOOK.COM

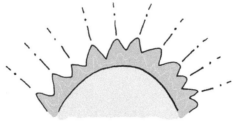

hello!

WE'RE SO GLAD YOU'RE HERE. YOU'RE ABOUT TO EMBARK ON A SELF-DISCOVERY JOURNEY ALONG THE RAINBOW ROAD.

DID YOU KNOW? RAINBOWS APPEAR WHEN LIGHT SHINES THROUGH WATER, CREATING BEAUTIFUL COLORS AS THE LIGHT IS BENT AND REFLECTED—JUST LIKE A MIRROR SHOWS YOUR REFLECTION!

THINK OF THIS BOOK AS AN INNER RAINBOW THAT WILL HELP YOU UNDERSTAND YOURSELF BETTER. EACH DAY, YOU'LL COMPLETE A MINDFULNESS ACTIVITY. ONCE YOU TAKE THREE TRIPS ALONG THE RAINBOW ROAD, YOU'LL RECEIVE YOUR POT OF GOLD.

ARE YOU READY TO START YOUR ADVENTURE?

DAY 1

IF YOU CAN DREAM IT, YOU CAN DO IT!

YOU HAVE THREE WEEKS TO GET TO THE END OF YOUR RAINBOW.
WHAT WILL BE YOUR TREASURE?

WRITE YOUR DREAMS IN THE RAINBOW BELOW.

dAY 2

EVERYTHING YOU CAN IMAGINE IS REAL.

– PABLO PICASSO

EVERYTHING BEGINS INSIDE OF US. BUT SOMETIMES IT CAN BE HARD
TO SHOW OUR TRUE COLORS.

USE THIS PAGE TO EXPRESS YOURSELF BY COLORING IN OUR
MANDALA WE CREATED JUST FOR YOU.

SELF CONFIDENCE IS A SUPER POWER. ONCE YOU START TO BELIEVE IN YOURSELF — MAGIC HAPPENS.

WHAT ARE YOU GREAT AT DOING?
WHAT WILL MOTIVATE YOU TO BE YOUR BEST SELF?
WHO INSPIRES YOU?

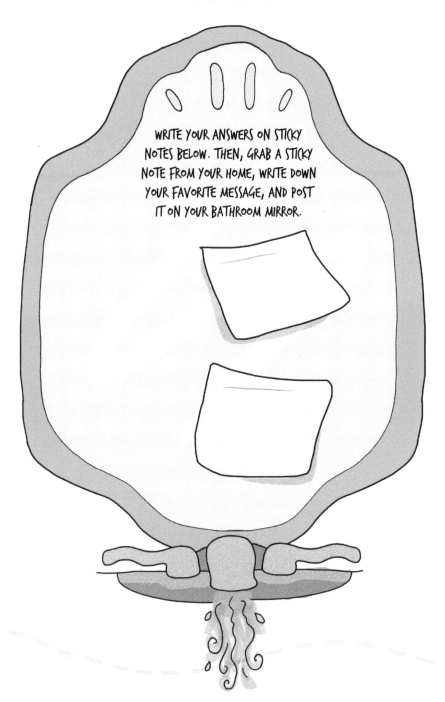

DAY 4

SELF CARE ISN'T SELFISH.

TAKING TIME FOR YOURSELF IS AN IMPORTANT MINDFULNESS PRACTICE. HOW CAN YOU GIVE YOURSELF SOME SELF CARE TODAY? WRITE IN THE BATH BUBBLES — THEN MAYBE ENJOY A BUBBLE BATH OF YOUR OWN!

DAY 5

ONE SIMPLE THOUGHT IN THE MORNING CAN CHANGE YOUR ENTIRE DAY.

HOW YOU TALK TO YOURSELF EACH DAY CAN MAKE A
BIG DIFFERENCE!

SOMETIMES, OUR INNER BULLY IS LOUD! THIS INNER BULLY TELLS
US LIES THAT WE AREN'T GOOD ENOUGH, CAPABLE OF DOING
THINGS, AND SO MUCH MORE.

INNER BULLY

OUR INNER TEACHER, ON THE OTHER HAND, ENCOURAGES US
TO LEARN NEW THINGS AND TRY OUR BEST. WHAT ARE THREE
THINGS YOUR INNER TEACHER WOULD SAY TO YOU?

INNER TEACHER

1.

2.

3.

DAY 6

IT IS GOOD TO LOOK AT THE PAST TO GAIN APPRECIATION FOR THE PRESENT AND PERSPECTIVE FOR THE FUTURE.

— GORDON B. HINCKLEY

WE ALL HOLD MEMORIES IN OUR HEARTS FROM PAST EXPERIENCES. DRAW OR WRITE ABOUT A SPECIAL MEMORY IN YOUR LIFE.

DAY 7

A MIRROR IS WHERE WE FIND A REFLECTION OF OUR APPEARANCES, BUT IN A HEART IS WHERE WE FIND A REFLECTION OF OUR SOULS.

CONGRATULATIONS! YOU'VE COMPLETED ONE FULL WEEK OF MINDFULNESS PRACTICES. HOW DO YOU FEEL?

TAKE A FEW MINUTES TO WRITE YOUR FEELINGS BELOW OR TELL A LOVED ONE ABOUT YOUR FIRST WEEK.

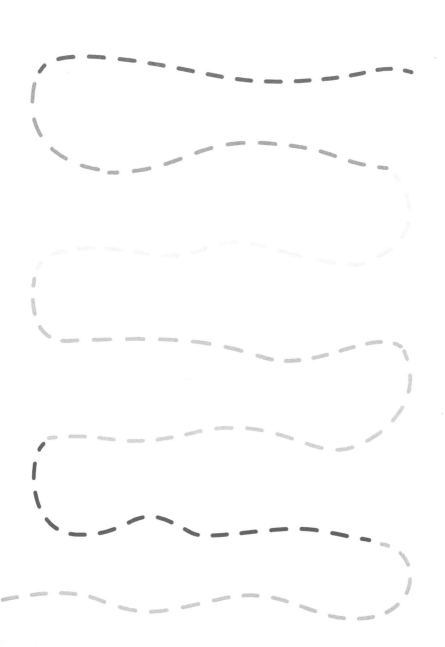

DAY 8

TO WALK IN NATURE IS TO WITNESS A
THOUSAND MIRACLES.

– MARY DAVIS

TAKE A WALK OUTSIDE. GRAB A GROWN-UP AND EXPLORE YOUR
NEIGHBORHOOD, SCHOOL PLAYGROUND OR YOUR OWN BACKYARD.
OF COURSE, IF IT'S COLD OR RAINY TODAY, YOU CAN TAKE AN
ADVENTURE WALK INSIDE.

DAY 9

CREATE WITH YOUR HEART, BUILD WITH YOUR MIND.

– CRISS JAMI

IMAGINE YOU ARE WALKING THROUGH A MAGICAL GARDEN.
DRAW WHAT YOU SEE.

STAND STRONG IN YOUR TRUE SELF.

TRY THESE POWERFUL POSES, HOLDING EACH FOR THREE BREATHS.
HOW DID YOU FEEL?

DAY 11

IF WE ALL DO ONE RANDOM ACT OF KINDNESS DAILY, WE MIGHT JUST SET THE WORLD IN THE RIGHT DIRECTION.

— MARTIN KORNFELD

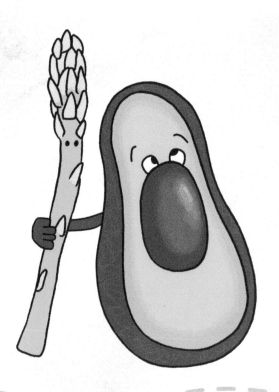

WHAT CAN YOU DO TO BRIGHTEN SOMEONE ELSE'S DAY TODAY?
WRITE IN A FEW RANDOM ACTS OF KINDNESS IN THE FACES
BELOW. THEN, PRACTICE YOUR RANDOM ACTS OF KINDNESS WITH
YOUR FRIENDS, FAMILY, AND EVERYONE YOU MEET!

DAY 12

BRAVELY BE YOU.

LAST WEEK, YOU LEARNED HOW TO LISTEN TO YOUR INNER TEACHER AND QUIET YOUR INNER CRITIC. ANY TIME YOUR INNER CRITIC GETS A LITTLE LOUD, REPEAT "I AM BRAVE."

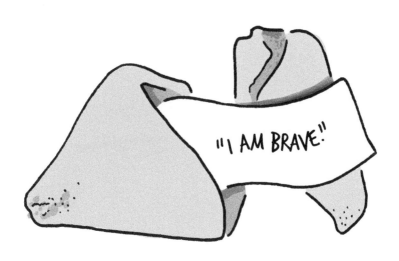

REFLECT: WHAT WILL THIS MANTRA HELP YOU DO?

_____

_____

_____

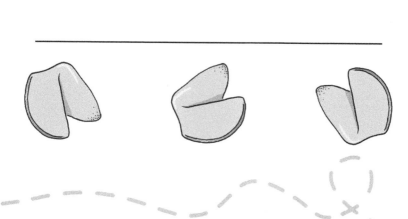

DAY 13

YESTERDAY IS HISTORY. TOMORROW IS A MYSTERY. TODAY IS A GIFT, THAT'S WHY THEY CALL IT THE PRESENT.

— ELEANOR ROOSEVELT

LAST WEEK, YOU REFLECTED ON THE PAST. TODAY, WE ENCOURAGE YOU TO EMBRACE THE PRESENT. LOOK AROUND THE ROOM YOU'RE IN. DRAW OR WRITE ABOUT ALL THAT IS AROUND YOU AND HOW YOU FEEL INSIDE.

DAY 14

REFLECTION IS LOOKING BACK SO THAT THE
VIEW LOOKING FORWARD IS EVEN CLEARER.

TWO WEEKS OF MINDFULNESS PRACTICES DOWN — YOU'RE OUT OF THIS WORLD!

REFLECT: WHAT HAS BEEN THE MOST CHALLENGING THING YOU'VE DONE SO FAR ON THIS JOURNEY? TAKE A FEW MINUTES TO TELL A LOVED ONE OR SHARE YOUR THOUGHTS BELOW.

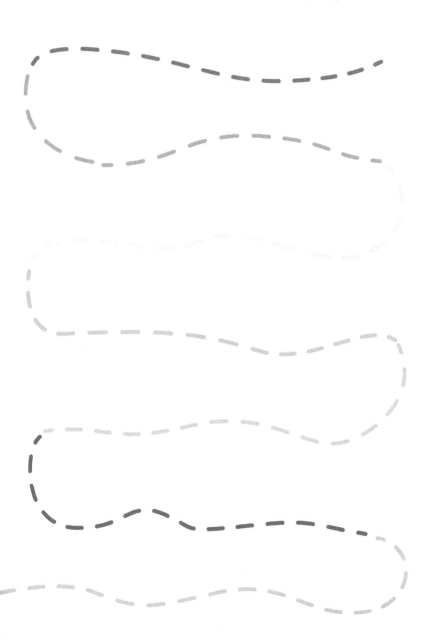

DAY 15

BEING STILL DOESN'T MEAN DON'T MOVE. IT MEANS MOVE IN PEACE.

– EYEN E. GARDNER

LAST WEEK, YOU TOOK A NATURE WALK. TODAY, IT'S TIME TO CREATE YOUR OWN NATURE MANDALA.

GATHER STICKS, LEAVES, ROCKS, AND MORE TO CREATE YOUR OWN OR SIMPLY COLOR IN THE PICTURE BELOW.

ATTACH A PHOTO OF YOUR MANDALA TO THIS PAGE!

DAY 16

MAKE VISIBLE WHAT, WITHOUT YOU, MIGHT PERHAPS NEVER HAVE BEEN SEEN.

– ROBERT BRESSON

EACH OF US HAS OUR OWN SUPERPOWERS INSIDE. ONLY YOU CAN CREATE WHAT'S INSIDE YOU. IT WILL BE DIFFERENT FROM YOUR FRIENDS, YOUR TEACHERS, AND FAMILY MEMBERS — AND THAT'S THE BEAUTY OF CREATIVITY! DON'T HOLD BACK...CREATE!

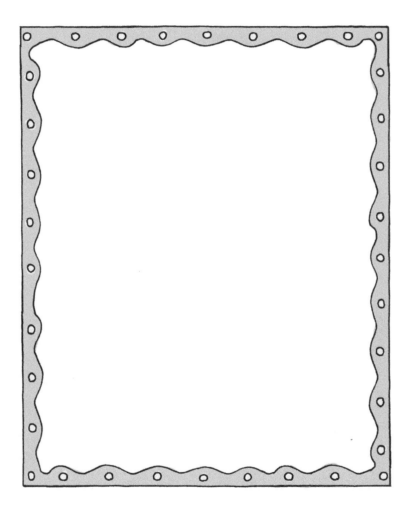

CONFIDENCE IS THE WILLINGNESS TO TRY.

— MEL ROBBINS

DAY 18

BE A RAINBOW IN SOMEONE ELSE'S CLOUD.

- MAYA ANGELOU

WHO IN YOUR LIFE COULD USE A RAINBOW OF JOY? WRITE A
LETTER TO THEM TO BRIGHTEN THEIR DAY.

DAY 19

ALWAYS SPEAK YOUR TRUTH, EVEN IF YOUR
VOICE SHAKES.

— MAGGIE KUHN

LAST WEEK, YOU PRACTICED YOUR "I AM BRAVE" MANTRA. TODAY,
CREATE YOUR OWN! WHAT WILL YOU LIVE BY TODAY?
FILL IN THE BLANK:

DAY 20

BE THE CHANGE YOU WISH TO SEE IN THE WORLD.

— MAHATMA GANDHI

YOU HAVE THE POWER TO CREATE YOUR WORLD AROUND YOU.

SPEND A FEW MINUTES DREAMING UP HOW YOU WILL CREATE
THE BEST FUTURE FOR YOURSELF, OTHERS, AND THE WORLD.

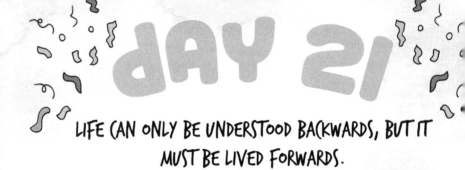

DAY 21

LIFE CAN ONLY BE UNDERSTOOD BACKWARDS, BUT IT MUST BE LIVED FORWARDS.

— SOREN KIERKEGAARD

CONGRATULATIONS! YOU'VE MADE IT TO THE END OF THE RAINBOW. WAY TO GO!

BEFORE THE CELEBRATIONS BEGIN, TAKE A FEW MINUTES TO REFLECT ON YOUR JOURNEY. TELL A LOVED ONE OR WRITE DOWN YOUR THOUGHTS HERE.

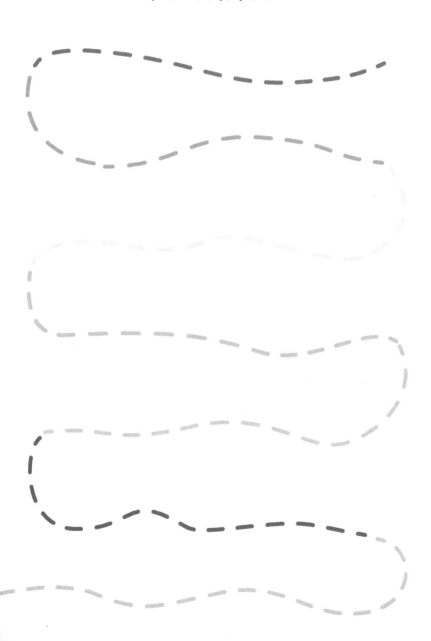

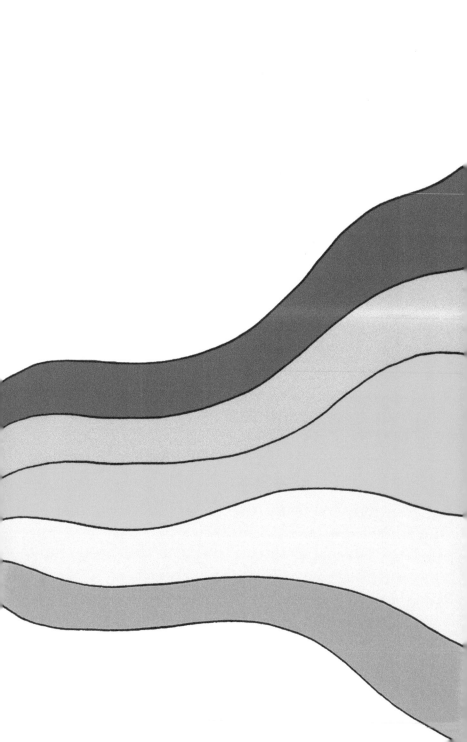

YOU MADE IT TO THE END OF THE RAINBOW ROAD.
ARE YOU READY FOR YOUR POT OF GOLD?

GUESS WHAT...YOU ARE ALREADY THE POT OF GOLD
YOU WERE SEARCHING FOR! YOU HAD THE MAGIC INSIDE
OF YOU ALL ALONG. ALL YOU HAD TO DO WAS TAKE
TIME EACH DAY TO DISCOVER YOUR INNER STRENGTH.

SHINE BRIGHTLY!

WANT TO CONTINUE YOUR MINDFULNESS JOURNEY? ASK
A PARENT TO HELP YOU VISIT OUR WEBSITE. THERE'S
SO MUCH MORE TO EXPLORE!

JOURNEYTOMEBOOK.COM

CPSIA information can be obtained
at www.ICGtesting.com
Printed in the USA
LVHW052205270121
677519LV00008B/271

9 781970 063868